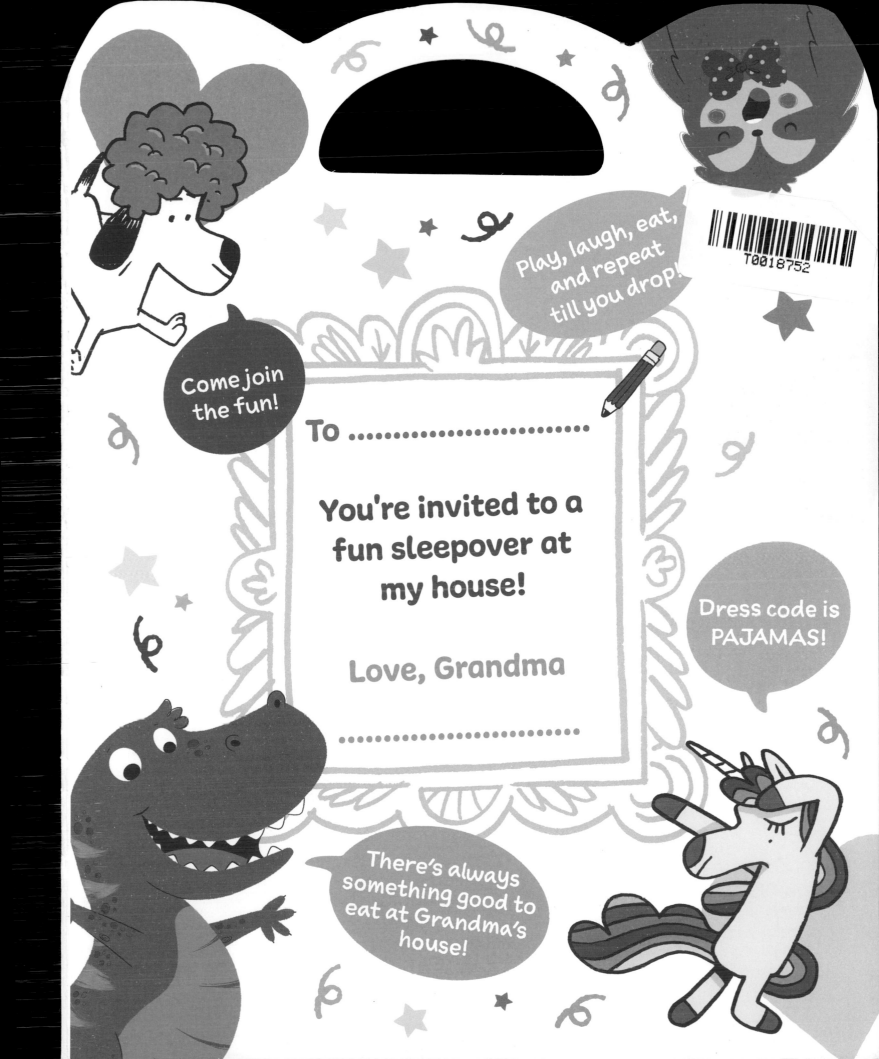

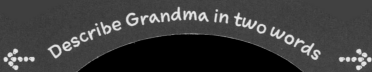
Describe Grandma in two words

MY GRANDMA'S HOME SWEET HOME

My favorite toy at Grandma's house is
....

Here's a picture of my Grandma and me!

Books I like to read at my Grandma's house
....
....

Decorate with some colorful stickers!

My favorite room at Grandma's house is

....

The best place to make a tent at my Grandma's house is

....

Here's a picture of my Grandma's house

Here's a picture of my tent at Grandma's house

Games I like to play with my Grandma

....

....

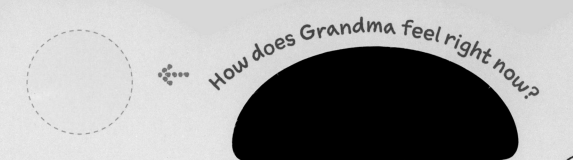

How does Grandma feel right now?

ALL ABOUT MY
GRANDMA

I call her ....,

and sometimes she calls me ....

She is .... years old.

Color the love heart!

She and I love to

....

She always says

....

I Love You Grandma

She makes the very best

....

I love the way she

....

Stick letters here

I L O V E M Y G R A N D M A

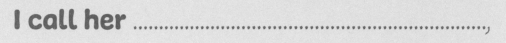

THIS IS ME

ALL ABOUT ME

I am .... years old.

I like ....

....

....

I don't like ....

....

Some of my favorite

things are ....

....

My favorite memory of

my Grandma and me is

....

....

....

....

Take a hike **OR** go for a swim?

Be really fast **OR** be really strong?

GRANDMA, WOULD YOU RATHER...?

Eat fruit **OR** vegetables?

Be friends with a unicorn **OR** a dinosaur?

Stay indoors **OR** go outdoors?

Sing **OR** dance?

Live on the Moon OR live on Mars?

Have spaghetti for hair OR fish for fingers?

Own a cat OR a dog?

Be able to fly OR travel through time?

Take a nap OR go for a walk?

Turn invisible OR read minds?

Jump in a pool of pudding OR a pool filled with jelly?

Now it's Grandma's turn to ask you!

Choose a path to follow and tell Grandma a story.

STORY PATH
WITH MY GRANDOMA

START

Now it's Grandma's turn to tell you a story!

THE END

9

Color in these silly sweet treats

My recipe for a perfect Grandma

Fill in all the secret ingredients and then color it in

A cup of ....

A tablespoon of ....

A drop of ....

A sprinkle of ....

A teaspoon of ....

A dash of ....

Mix together with ....

Add a pinch of ....

A drop of ....

A teaspoon of ....

Bake.

Serve with ....

Made with love from ....

YUM!

ADD YOUR NAME

BATHTIME BRAINTEASER

Ask Grandma to help you find the letter stickers to fill in the grid.

WOW

SOAP
TAP
WATER
BUBBLES
BRUSH

~~TOWEL~~
RUBBER DUCK
SHAMPOO
SPONGE

9 **T O W E L**

Decorate with giggling animal stickers

Knock Knock.
Who's there?
Boo.
Boo who?
Don't cry Grandma, it's only a joke.

KNOCK KNOCK, GRANDMA

Knock Knock.
Who's there?
Hawaii.
Hawaii who?
I'm fine Grandma, how are you?

HA HA!

Knock Knock.
Who's there?
Beets.
Beets who?
Beets me!

Knock Knock.
Who's there?
Wa.
Wa who?
What are you excited about?!

Knock Knock.
Who's there?
Shelby.
Shelby who?
Shelby coming 'round the mountain when she comes.

HA HA!

Knock Knock.
Who's there?
Cows go.
Cows go who?
No Grandma, cows
go MOOOOOO!!!

Knock Knock.
Who's there?
Icing.
Icing who?
Icing so loudly so
everyone can
hear me!

Knock Knock.
Who's there?
Lettuce.
Lettuce who?
Lettuce in!

Knock Knock.
Who's there?
Spell.
Spell who?
W-H-O !

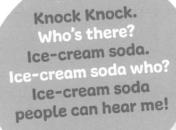

Knock Knock.
Who's there?
Ice-cream soda.
Ice-cream soda who?
Ice-cream soda
people can hear me!

Knock Knock.
Who's there?
Justin.
Justin who?
Justin time
for dinner,
Grandma.

Ask Grandma to write a joke

Knock Knock.
Who's there?

Write your own joke

Knock Knock.
Who's there?

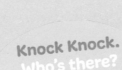

Knock Knock.
Who's there?
Lena.
Lena who?
Lena a little closer,
and I'll tell you
another joke!

LOL!

MY GRANDOMA'S Scavenger Hunt

What can you find around Grandma's house?

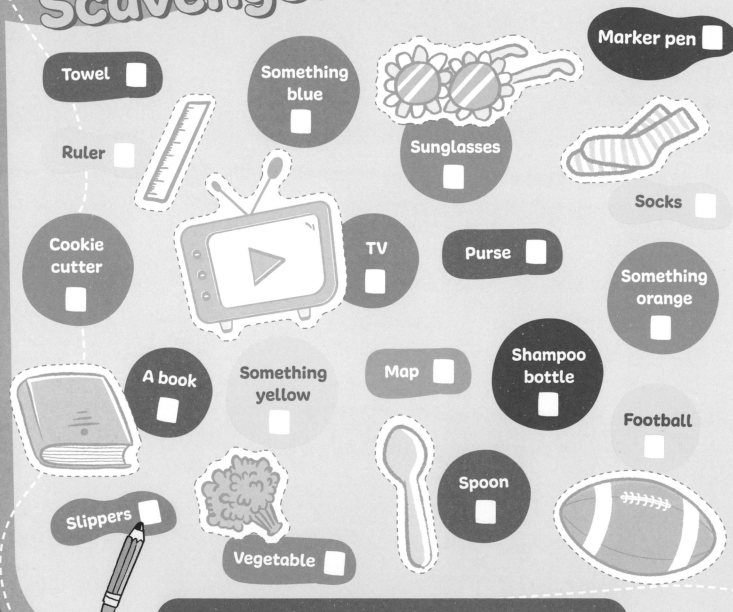

Marker pen ☐

Towel ☐

Something blue ☐

Sunglasses ☐

Ruler ☐

Socks ☐

Cookie cutter ☐

TV ☐

Purse ☐

Something orange ☐

A book ☐

Something yellow ☐

Map ☐

Shampoo bottle ☐

Football ☐

Slippers ☐

Vegetable ☐

Spoon ☐

Add the stickers, and then check the box when you've found each item!

Cup ☐

Clock ☐

Money ☐

Fruit ☐

Remote ☐

Toothbrush ☐

Something
green ☐

Camera ☐

Something
soft ☐

Candle ☐

Toy ☐

Colored
pencils ☐

Backpack ☐

Plant ☐

Candy ☐

Something
that makes
a noise ☐

Something
red ☐

Hairbrush ☐

How many items did you find? ☐ ☐

17

Ask Grandma to give you a score out of 10

Color in me and my friends!

My favorite dance song is

19

MY GRANDMA'S SPECIAL MENU

Draw the favorite meals that Grandma always cooks for you.

MY SUPER GRANDMA
AND SUPER ME!

Draw super Grandma
and her superhero
gadgets

WOW!

Super ID

Stick photo here

My Grandma's superhero name:

My Grandma's super powers:

- [ ] Bravery
- [ ] Invisibility
- [ ] Strength
- [ ] X-ray vision
- [ ] Helps others
- [ ]

ADD YOUR OWN

Now draw yourself
as a superhero

Don't forget your
superhero gadgets!

Super ID

Stick
photo
here

My superhero name:

My super powers:

- ☐ Bravery
- ☐ Invisibility
- ☐ Strength
- ☐ X-ray vision
- ☐ Helps others
- ☐ ADD YOUR OWN

BAM!

KA-POW!

THE .... FAMILY TREE

Draw your family.

♥ MEET MY ♥

AWESOME FAMILY

24

STICKER FUN

sweet

FUN

KIND

Huggable

SILLY

BEST GRANDMA IN THE WORLD

SUPER STAR

Page 13

GOOD JOB!

WOW

Pages 14-15

SLEEPOVERS ROCK!

A A A A A A A A A A A A A A B

B B B B B B B B B B B B C C C C C C C C C C C ! E

B 0 1 2 3 4 5 6 7 8 9 0 1 2 3 4 5 6 7 !

C C C C C C D D D D D D E E E E E E E E E

STICKER FUN

SHHHH
I'm still asleep

HI!

YO!

COOL

E E E E F F F F F F F F F F F F G G G G G G G G G G G G

I I I I I I J J J J J J J J J K K K K K K

G H H H H H H H H H H H H H I I I I I I I ? K

H 8 9 0 1 2 3 4 5 6 7 8 9 0 1 2 3 4 5 ? K

STICKER FUN

Pages 22-23

Pages 26-27

Page 31

KA-POW!

WOW!

BAM!

Pages 32-33

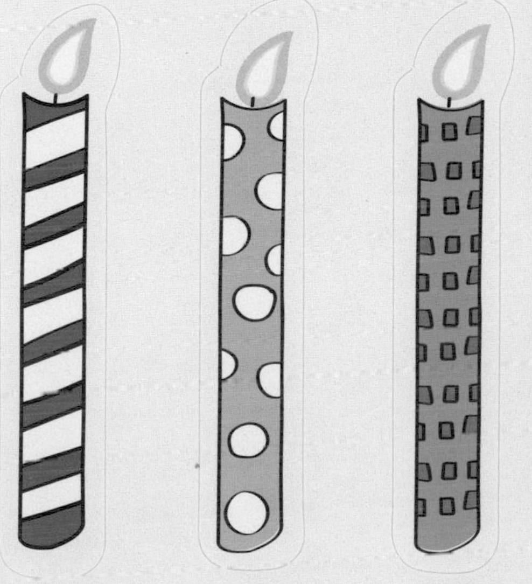

Pages 38-39

L L L L L L L L L M M M M M M M M M M N N N

O O O O O O P P P P P P P P Q Q Q Q R R R R R R R R P

N N N N O O O O O O O O O O O O O O !
N 6 7 8 9 0 1 2 3 4 5 6 7 8 9 1 2 3 4 !

STICKER FUN

OMG

BFF

AWESOME

FEELING SLEEP-PEA zzz

BEE HAPPY

I ♥ DADDY

BEAR-LY AWAKE
DO NOT DISTURB

Dream On

DINO-SNORE TIME!

I ♥ GRANDPA

I ♥ YOU

LOL!

I ♥ MOMMY

YOU SNOOZE YOU LOSE zzz

I'M HAPPY

T-REST TIME

NEED MORE SLEEP

I AM SNORE-SOME

HAVING A WHALE OF A TIME

PLAY LAUGH EAT SLEEP REPEAT

SUPER ME!!!!!!!!

I ♥ GRANDMA

R R R R R R R R S S S S S S S S S S S S S

V V V V V V W W W W W W X X Y Y Y Y Z Z Z

S T T T T T T T T T T T T T U U U U U U U ? Z

S 5 6 7 8 9 0 1 2 3 4 5 6 7 8 9 0 0 0 ? Z

Draw your family pets.

Movie Sleepover Checklist

Plan your magical movie sleepover party with Grandma!

Supplies
Check the box, then add some color.

Snacks ☐

Drinks ☐

Music ☐

Games ☐

Pet animal or a toy one! ☐

Pajamas ☐

Bedtime books ☐

Cushions ☐

Slippers ☐

Blankets ☐

POP

Schedule
Fill in the time

_____ PM **Play a game**

_____ PM Watch a movie from your list

_____ PM Share stories about the movie

_____ PM Snuggles with Grandma!

_____ PM Read a book to Grandma

_____ PM Lights out for you and Grandma!

My Top 5 Movies to watch with Grandma

1 _____

2 _____

3 _____

4 _____

5 _____

I SPY
WITH MY GRANDMA

What can you see?

Draw all the things you and Grandma spot on your next trip outdoors.

Draw your dream pets

PETS WE LOVE

Color in the turtle!

30

My Grandma's dream pet is

....

Draw your favorite pet!

My dream pet is

....

Find your pet stickers. Then, can you draw a line to match each pet with its shadow?

1

2

3

4

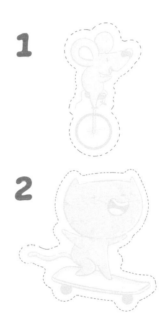
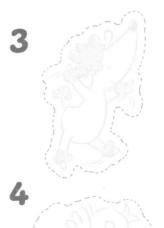

A

B

C

D

MY GRANDMA'S
BAKE-OFF
Color in Grandma's yummy cakes!

Don't forget to stick the candles on!

Draw your favorite cupcake

Our favorite toppings

- [ ] Candy sprinkles
- [ ] Chocolate chips
- [ ] Chopped candy bars
- [ ] Strawberries
- [ ] Banana
- [ ] Shredded coconut
- [ ] Sugar candies
- [ ] Mini marshmallows
- [ ] ....
- [ ] ....

Ask Grandma to draw her favorite cupcake

33

COLOR BY NUMBERS

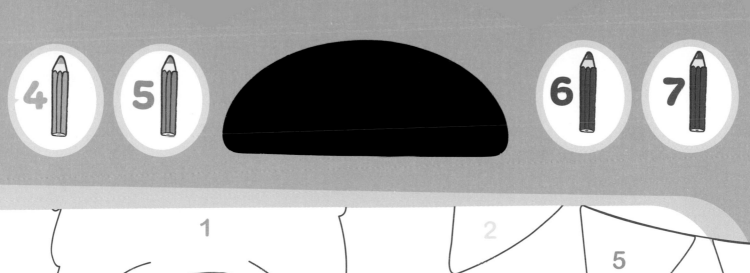

Draw pictures for Grandma's fridge.

GRANDMA AND

Use your letter stickers to write your name

My Top 5 treats at Grandma's house:

1 ....

2 ....

3 ....

4 ....

5 ....

Super kiwi!

Yip-pea!

Snack monster!

Decorate your drawings with some fun stickers!

SILLY SLEEPOVER STORY

Fill in the missing words to create a fun story about you and Grandma's special time together.

On a bright and sunny morning, Grandma and ....

▲ ADD YOUR NAME

went on a fun day out to the ....
▲ (Where do you want to go?)

Along the way, they saw something totally out of this world.

It was a .... in a ....
▲ (Choose an animal)   ▲ (Choose a vehicle)

"Oh my!" said Grandma. "Look, now it's eating ....
▲ (Choose a snack)

from a ...." Then the ....
▲ (Choose a funny thing for it to eat from)   ▲ (Animal you chose earlier)

in the .... raced off.
▲ (Vehicle you chose earlier)

ZOOOM!

They followed the .... all the way to the ....
▲ (Animal you chose earlier)   ▲ (Place you want to visit)

38

where they also spotted a ....
▲ (Make up a funny animal)

wearing ....,
▲ (Choose an item of clothing)

and playing ....
▲ (Choose a musical instrument)

The noise was louder than ....
▲ (Choose something that makes Grandma cover her ears)

ADD YOUR NAME

Grandma and .... had the funniest day ever, and they laughed

all the way home, dreaming of their next big adventure.

Maybe they'll go ....
▲ (Choose another place to visit)

THE END

GRANDMA'S
WISHES FOR ME

MY WISHES
FOR GRANDMA

ANIMAL STARGAZING

Join the stars and color in the fun animal constellations!

Canis Major means "The Greater Dog."

See if you and Grandma can spot these stars in the night sky!

Piscis Austrinus means "The Southern Fish."

NIGHT

Carefully color in all the stars.

NIGHT WITH MY GRANDMA

There are ☐☐ stars.

ODD ONE OUT

1

2

3

4

5

6

7

8

9

Can you and Grandma find the odd hat that doesn't make a pair?

ANSWER 7